THE BUCK STOPS HERE

THE BUCK STOPS HERE

A BIOGRAPHY OF HARRY TRUMAN

A People in Focus Book

By Morrie Greenberg

dP DILLON PRESS, INC.
Minneapolis, Minnesota 55415

Library of Congress Cataloging-in-Publication Data

Greenberg, Morrie.
The buck stops here : a biography of Harry Truman / by Morrie
Greenberg.
(People in focus)
Bibliography: p.
Includes index.
Summary: Traces the life and career of the statesman, from his birth
and early life in Missouri, to his days in Washington, D.C. as a
senator and president, to his retirement.
ISBN 0-87518-394-8

1. Truman, Harry S., 1884-1972—Juvenile literature. 2. Presidents—United States—Biography—Juvenile literature. [1. Truman, Harry S., 1884-1972. 2. Presidents.] I. Title. II. Series:
People in focus book.
E814.G74   1989
973.917'092'4—dc 19
[B]
[92]   88-20264
                                                       CIP
                                                       AC

Dillon Press, Inc., 242 Portland Avenue South
Minneapolis, Minnesota 55415

Printed in the United States of America
   2 3 4 5 6 7 8 9 10 98 97 96 95 94 93 92 91 90

To Audrey

Photographic Acknowledgments

Photographs have been reproduced through the courtesy of the Harry S. Truman Library in Independence, Missouri. Special thanks to Pauline Testerman of the library's audio visual section; the Department of State; the *Kansas City Star*; the *Kansas City Journal Post*; J. Sherrel Lakey; Los Alamos National Laboratory; National Park Service/Abbie Rowe; Office of War Information; the Signal Corps; the U.S. Army; the U.S. Information Agency; and the U.S. Navy.

Contents

Chapter/One

A Whole New World

As soon as Vice-President Harry Truman walked into the large room on the second floor of the White House, he knew something was terribly wrong. Never had he seen Eleanor Roosevelt, the president's wife, looking so sad. Mrs. Roosevelt moved toward him and slowly placed her hand on his shoulder.

"Harry," she said, "the president is dead."

The vice-president stared at her, too stunned to answer. His eyes welled up with tears. He had to be certain that he heard her correctly. The president—dead? Finally, gathering his strength, he looked squarely at the First Lady.

"Is there anything I can do for you?" he asked.

Eleanor Roosevelt shook her head. "Is there

anything we can do for you?" she answered. "For you are the one in trouble now."

Harry Truman and President Franklin D. Roosevelt had been elected together only a few months before. What a great victory it had been for both of them, and for the Democratic party! When Truman heard about the president's death, he told a group of reporters: "I don't know whether you fellows ever had a load of hay fall on you, but. . .I felt like the moon, the stars, and all the planets had fallen on me."

Two and a half hours after President Roosevelt's death, on April 12, 1945, members of the president's cabinet and a few congressional leaders watched—silent, almost unbelieving—as Harry S. Truman placed his right hand on a Bible, and swore to "preserve, protect, and defend the Constitution of the United States, so help me God," as the nation's thirty-third president.

Americans were crushed by the news of the president's death. Roosevelt had been president for over twelve years—longer than any president in history. He had given Americans hope and courage during the Great Depression of the 1930s, and had led the country through the darkest days of World War II. Now that he was gone, people worried about the future of the United States.

The war in Europe was almost over, but the war with Japan might drag on for months or years. What would a new president do to get Japan to surrender? Would he know how to make the right kind of peace agreements?

Who was Harry S. Truman? Many people had never heard of him before he was nominated as vice-president. Truman looked and acted so ordinary, and spoke with a jarring, flat twang. He didn't have a college degree. Americans had many questions and concerns about the new president.

Harry S. Truman was born on the morning of May 8, 1884. When the country doctor told John Truman that his wife Martha had given birth to a baby boy, the proud Missouri farmer shook the doctor's hand, carefully counted out the fifteen-dollar fee, and then—hammer and nails in hand—headed for the front door. Once outside, the beaming father, also a mule and horse trader, nailed a good-luck horseshoe firmly in place above the door of the small frame house. The horseshoe signaled to friends and neighbors in the small village that John and Martha Truman were the proud parents of a baby boy—their first child. Besides, the young farmer and his wife needed all the good luck they could get.

The Trumans named their baby boy Harry, after his uncle Harrison Young. The new parents had a little more trouble deciding on a middle name. Should they make it Shippe for John's father, Anderson Shippe Truman, or Solomon for Martha's father, Solomon Young? After some thought, they hit upon the answer. They named their son Harry S. Truman, and the "S" would stand for both grandfathers.

John Truman had married Martha Ellen Young two and a half years before, in Grandview, Missouri. A year later, they moved to Lamar, a small village where John hoped to trade and sell animals to the farmers around the area. However, horseshoe or no horseshoe, Harry Truman's father had little luck with his trading business.

The Trumans moved from one small village in western Missouri to another as John Truman tried to make a living. By the time little Harry was four years old, the Truman family had moved—taking unsold horses and mules along—from Lamar to Harrisonville to Belton and then back to Grandview. In Grandview the Trumans lived on the family farm owned by Martha's parents, Grandfather and Grandmother Young.

When Harry was six years old, the Truman family moved to a house in Independence, Mis-

Harry Truman's parents, Martha Ellen Young and John Anderson Truman, on their wedding day.

souri, because Harry's mother believed that the schools in this larger town were better than the country schools near Grandview. Educating her children was very important to Martha Truman. She herself had received a strong education in music and art from a women's college in Missouri.

Moving all the time didn't seem to bother Harry. He was a bright, happy boy who generally did what he was told. By this time, Harry had a younger brother, Vivian, who was three, and a baby sister, Mary Jane, who was one year old.

Independence was unlike any of the tiny Missouri towns in which the Trumans had previously lived. Home to more than six thousand people, Independence was a quiet town with an exciting history—it had once been the busy starting point for travelers from the East heading to New Mexico, Utah, or California, from the 1840s to the 1860s. Harry loved to listen to Grandfather Young tell stories about how he drove wagon trains west from Independence in those days.

Harry liked to take in the sights of the town. Banks, saloons, and a department store surrounded a public square paved with asphalt. Horses hitched to farm wagons or buggies clumped through the streets. The town had the most beautiful homes Harry had ever seen.

Harry, at age four, stands to the right of his two-year-old brother, Vivian.

Harry's mother, however, began to wonder how much Harry could actually see. Before Harry was five, she had sat with him and taught him how to read the family Bible with its large letters. Harry was bright and eager to learn, but when he picked up other books, he soon discovered that the print was too small for him to read.

As the problem grew worse, his mother took Harry to an eye doctor in nearby Kansas City who fitted him with a pair of thick glasses. The new glasses changed Harry's life tremendously. Because he was afraid of breaking his glasses, he now kept away from the rough-and-tumble games that the other boys played. Some of the children started calling him "Four Eyes" since it was so unusual to see a six year old wearing glasses in those days. The glasses may have kept Harry from doing many of the things he wanted to do, but they also opened up a whole new world for him. Now that he could read the small print in books, he could read anything!

The Independence Library had two large, high-ceilinged rooms lined with more than two thousand books. Little Harry soon became a regular visitor. In fact, he claimed to have read every book in the Independence Library—including the encyclopedias—by the time he graduated from high

One of Truman's elementary school classes in Independence, Missouri. Harry is the first boy on the left in the front row, and is holding his glasses in his hand.

school. History books and biographies were his favorites. Harry liked to tell people that he was so busy reading books that he didn't have time to get into trouble.

As Harry grew older, he was either reading, helping with chores around the house, working at a part-time job at a drugstore, or practicing on the family piano. He loved music. From the time he was ten until he was fifteen (when he decided that playing the piano made him a "sissy"), Harry practiced two hours a day and took music lessons once a week.

Reading and music were important to him, but

Harry Truman at fifteen years old.

according to Harry, Elizabeth Virginia Wallace, nicknamed Bess, was even more important. He first saw her "yellow curls and blue eyes" in Sunday school when he was six, and she was five. Even though he felt strongly about her from the beginning, it took Harry five years before he got up enough nerve to speak to her. He sat in front of Bess in the sixth and seventh grade and on into high school. Once in a while, she let him carry her books home. Harry never stopped believing that Bess was the girl for him, but small town customs kept the two of them far apart.

Bess's well-to-do family lived in a beautiful home on Delaware Street. Her friends were boys and girls from the fashionable part of Independence. Harry, on the other hand, came from a family of plain, hard-working farmers. Although Harry did not fit in with the "fashionable" crowd, he hoped that someday Bess would care for him anyway.

Chapter/Two

A Chance Meeting

Harry and Bess graduated from Independence High School in 1901. He wanted to go on to college, but that would take money that his family did not have. Harry did have one hope, however. If he could get into the West Point Military Academy, he could become an army officer and get a free college education at the same time. Harry and a friend began to study together to get into the academy. One day, when he was visiting in Kansas City, he stopped by a recruiting station. The officer behind the desk told him that he needed perfect eyesight to get into West Point. That was the end of Harry's West Point idea.

At about this time, Harry's father was barely making enough money to support the Truman fam-

In this Independence High School "Class of 1901" photo, Truman is fourth from the left in the back row. Bess Wallace is on the far right in the second row.

ily. He had invested in the grain futures market, but when the price of grain dropped quickly and dramatically, John Truman lost the family home and most of his money. It was a sad day for the Trumans.

The family moved to Kansas City, Missouri. Anxious to keep his brother and sister in school, young Harry found a summer job working as a timekeeper with the Santa Fe Railroad. He kept track of the hours worked by men who were grading the railroad land. Harry—fresh out of high school—picked up a crude but colorful vocabulary from the down-to-earth railroad workers.

Later, he began working as a bank clerk at a Kansas City bank. Though he didn't like what he

considered to be a boring job, he kept it for
four years—doing his best and never complaining.
"You'll notice," Truman once said, "that the work
of the world gets done by people who aren't belly-
achers."

The job of bank clerk didn't seem to keep
Harry busy enough. At the age of twenty-one, he
volunteered to serve in a Missouri National Guard
field artillery unit that was stationed in Kansas
City. He served as a "part-time soldier" for three
years, and later volunteered for another three-year
hitch.

In 1906, bad luck hit the Trumans again. Harry's father's small farm washed away during a
flood. When Harry's Uncle Harrison Young retired, however, the Trumans were offered the opportunity to take over the Youngs' six-hundred-
acre farm in Grandview, Missouri. Harry's father
now needed help to run such a large farm, and he
asked Harry to leave Kansas City to come help
him. Harry agreed. He had never done any real
farming before, and the neighbors wondered if the
mild, bookish Harry would be able to take on such
hard work. They need not have worried.

Up at 4:30 A.M. in the summer and 6:30 in the
winter, the bank clerk-turned-farmer plowed and
sowed the fields, fed the hogs, baled the hay, fixed

Harry Truman in his National Guard uniform.

Truman, his mother, and Grandmother Young pose in front of the Truman home and farm in Grandview, Missouri.

the fences, and tended sick animals. The neighbors agreed that Harry was about as good a farmer as could be found in Missouri. He was smart enough to rotate his crops and use the other techniques scientists advised farmers to use in the early 1900s.

One day, while Harry was working in the barn, one of his cousins came in and began telling him about the Masons, and about the men in this organization who worked for "brotherhood" and charity. Harry liked what his cousin told him, and so he joined a Masonic lodge in a town nearby. Later, he started a lodge in Grandview, and became the leader of all the Masons in Missouri.

Harry stayed on the Grandview farm from 1906 to 1917. He did not get rich, but he made enough money to help support himself and his family. Besides, there was something else Harry liked about farming. It gave him plenty of time to think.

On a summer day in 1910—on one of those rare days when he was not working on his farm—Harry sat visiting with his cousins in nearby Independence. His Aunt Ella remarked that she was going across the street to return a plate to the Wallace family.

The Wallace family!

Harry almost jumped out of his shoes. It had been nine years since high school graduation, nine years since he had seen Bess Wallace. His heartbeat quickened—time had not erased any of the wonderful memories Harry had of Bess. His work in Kansas City and then in Grandview had made it almost impossible for their paths to cross.

He would not let this opportunity slip by.

Harry grabbed the cake plate from his aunt's hands, stepped quickly out the door, and—as he half-walked, half-ran toward the house across the way—he called out that he would gladly save his aunt the trouble of returning the plate. Moments later, Harry Truman stood inside the spacious Wallace home staring at Bess. As he handed Bess the empty cake plate, and as Bess invited him to come in, he could not help but notice that Bess Wallace at twenty-five was just as beautiful and charming as he remembered her from their early school days. Harry spent the evening telling Bess what he had done since high school, and when it was time to say good-night, he asked Bess if he could "come calling" again. Bess told him politely that he could.

Traveling from the Grandview farm to Independence in those days meant a long walk, a train ride, another long walk, and a final streetcar ride. The two-to-four-hour trip, however, never seemed to dampen Harry Truman's feelings toward Bess. When work on the farm kept him from seeing Bess, he wrote her long letters. In the letters, he talked about many things—the hard farm work, books and magazines, music, or how his family was getting along. He always added how much he cared about her.

Ten months after he returned the cake plate, Harry got up enough courage to write to Bess and ask her if she would consider marrying him. He wrote, "You may not have guessed it, but I've been crazy about you since we went to Sunday school together. But I never had the nerve to think you'd even look at me. I don't think so now but I can't keep from telling you what I think of you."

Harry Truman riding a cultivator on the Grandview farm.

Harry knew that he was leading with his heart and not his head. Bess's mother, who had been a widow for seven years, made it perfectly clear how little she thought of the struggling dirt farmer who kept calling on her daughter. Marry my only daughter? she asked. Take Bess from our beautiful fourteen-room home to live the wretched life of a farmer's wife? Bess's mother felt that the Trumans and the Wallaces lived in two different worlds.

Bess tried to be kind. She told Harry that though she would not marry him, she still wanted to be friends. Harry seemed satisfied with just being able to keep on seeing Bess. Sometimes, Harry took Bess to the vaudeville theaters and restaurants in Kansas City. They went on long walks in the country, or took drives in the second-hand automobile Harry had bought in 1914.

Most of the time, however, Harry worked hard on the family farm in Grandview. Harry's burden grew when his younger brother, Vivian, got married and moved off the farm. The Trumans faced a terrible blow when John Truman injured himself trying to lift a large boulder, and died a few weeks later. All of the responsibility for running the farm now fell on Harry, his sister, and his mother.

Harry wanted to succeed at something besides farming. If he got rich, Bess and her mother might accept him. Truman's first money-making idea was to buy some cheap land in Texas, and sell it at a good profit. However, his rich uncle would not invest in his idea, which put an end to those plans. Refusing to give up, Truman borrowed $11,000 and invested it in a lead and zinc mining business in Oklahoma. He lost every cent. Finally, with money left to him by an uncle, he turned to the oil business and—once again—lost his money.

No matter how hard he tried, Harry Truman's hopes of winning Bess by getting rich seemed to be doomed to failure. "I seem to have a grand and admirable ability for calling tails when heads come up," he wrote Bess.

As the years passed, Bess grew fond of the farmer who knew how to make her laugh, who talked about the things that interested her most, who never stopped loving her, and who never stopped believing in himself. Three and a half years after Harry had returned the cake plate, Bess told Harry that if she married anyone, he would be the man. Three and a half years after that, in 1917, Bess said yes to Harry Truman. At last a date could be set for the wedding.

Or could it?

Across the ocean, Europe was at war. For many years, European countries had been building up their armies and competing with each other for trade and colonies. Finally, in 1914, when the Archduke of Austria-Hungary was shot and killed, Austria-Hungary blamed Serbia and declared war. Other countries began to take sides in the war, and soon the Allies—Great Britain, France, Russia, and other European countries—were at war with the Central Powers, which included Germany and Austria-Hungary. Harry followed the stories in the newspapers as World War I raged on. Terrible new weapons—poison gas, airplanes, machine guns, tanks, and huge cannons—were used to kill millions of people.

When the war began, President Woodrow Wilson had said that the United States would stay out of the war. However, as the war dragged on, remaining neutral became more and more difficult. Most of the people in the United States wanted the Allies to defeat the Central Powers, but this was not happening. Finally, when German submarines began to sink American ships without warning, the United States declared war on Germany on April 6, 1917.

Harry believed that it was his duty to enlist in the army. Many of the men he knew in the National Guard were volunteering. It wasn't an easy decision. If he went into the army, his sister would be the only one left in the family to run the large farm and take care of his aging mother. And it would be difficult to leave Bess, just when they had decided to get married.

When Bess heard that Harry had joined the army, she told him that she wanted to marry him before he went overseas. Harry was thirty-three—he had waited a long time for Bess—but he refused to marry her until he came back from the war. "I didn't think it was right to get married. . .and have the most beautiful girl and the sweetest girl in the world tied down," he said. After all, he might be wounded or even killed in the war.

Chapter/Three

Captain Harry

Before going overseas, Harry Truman dropped by the office of an optician in New York City. He bought two pairs of glasses, which brought his collection up to six pairs. Keeping so many pairs of glasses may have surprised the people who did not know Truman well, but it would not surprise his friends. He would never be caught fighting the war in Europe without being able to see where he was going.

When Harry was sworn into the National Guard, he thought he might have a chance of being elected a sergeant. In those days, the Guard elected its own officers. To Harry's surprise, he was instead elected a first lieutenant. He was pleased, but a little scared of the large responsibility. His regiment was

Harry Truman in France in World War I.

soon sent to Fort Sill, Oklahoma, for training. He enjoyed the time spent training to be an efficient soldier, as well as his experience running a successful army store.

In 1918, the 129th Field Artillery of the 35th Division was ordered to France. Soon after Harry arrived, Bess sent him a picture of herself with these words on the back: "May this photograph bring you safely home again from France—Bess." Harry carried the photo with him for the rest of the war.

Truman had his work cut out for him. One of the 35th Division's batteries, or groups of soldiers in the artillery, was called "Dizzy Battery D"—and with good reason. These tough, brawling men from some of the meanest neighborhoods in Kansas City enjoyed tormenting their officers. They hounded their first three commanders so much that one of them suffered a nervous breakdown. The soldiers were just waiting to tackle the next officer.

In July, Harry Truman, now a captain, was put in command of Battery D. He made up his mind that the men would not get the best of him. Yet, even in a captain's uniform, Truman was not exactly an impressive-looking leader. Although he was five feet nine inches tall, the captain with the thick glasses and slight build looked small.

This is the photo of Bess that Harry carried with him during World
War I.

Battery D put Captain Truman to the test on his first day of command. The men faked a stampede of their horses, and even started a free-for-all fight. What was the new captain going to do about it?

The corporals and sergeants of Battery D soon got the word—the captain wanted to see all of them at once. When they had all reported, Captain Truman told them that if any one of them could not keep discipline, he would be "busted" back to a private.

Every soldier left the meeting feeling that the captain meant business. It was not so much what he said, it was the way he said it. Truman felt satisfied that he had won the first round, but he knew that the real test of whether or not he could command his men would come later—in battle.

A month later, Captain Truman's artillery outfit was ordered to the front, and Battery D moved to a place called Mount Herrenberg, not far from the enemy line. Once his men were in position, Truman ordered them to fire a barrage of shells over a hill. The Germans answered with some shells of their own. One of the sergeants in Battery D panicked. He began yelling, "Run for your lives! Run for your lives!" A few of the men scrambled from their positions and began to run.

Captain Harry.

At this point, Captain Truman did a little yelling himself. When the fleeing members of Battery D heard all of the swearing and cursing coming from their slightly built captain, they quickly decided that it would be wiser to take their chances with the enemy than to cross an angry Harry Truman. They returned to their positions. If any of the other soldiers had thoughts of retreating that day, they reconsidered now as the blasts of the fiery captain still rang in their ears. Later, the regiment's chaplain, or clergyman, reported that the new captain's words "took the skin off the ears of those boys."

The soldiers of Company D would soon discover another side of Harry Truman. One day they were dragging their way to the St. Mihiel front through a hilly part of France, when the colonel of the regiment came riding by on horseback. He angrily demanded to know why the men were not moving faster, and accused them of loafing. Truman had put his own horse in a harness to help pull the artillery gun, and was trudging along with the men. He started to explain to the colonel that the men were very weary from a long march, but the colonel would not listen. He ordered Truman to make the men march double-time up a hill.

Instead, Truman ordered the soldiers to move

to some nearby woods and bed down. He knew how tired his men were. Going straight to the colonel, he said, "My men are not going to go any further. If you want to, go ahead and court-martial me."

The soldiers of Company D never forgot what Captain Truman did for them that day. Before long, they began to discover what kind of a man their captain really was. If a soldier had a problem or needed some help, he could always go see "Captain Harry." One Company D soldier summed it up when he said, "The men trusted him to get them through the war and to get them back home. And he went out of his way to help us."

The captain never thought of himself as a hero, but he did sense that he had proved himself as a leader in the war. He believed that a good leader is someone who can make people enjoy doing what they don't want to do. Truman learned that he could lead a group of difficult men and gain both their friendship and respect.

Truman spent almost exactly a year overseas. Germany signed an armistice (truce) agreement with the Allies, and, on November 11, 1918, the war ended. Almost nine million soldiers died in the war and nearly twenty-one million soldiers were wounded. World War I exhausted Europe, but it helped break down the power of Austria-Hungary and Germany.

In 1919, Truman returned to the United States and was discharged from the army as a major on May 6. Bess and Harry Truman were married on June 28. Harry was thirty-five, and Bess was a year younger. Nine years had passed since Harry had begun seeing Bess. Guests at the Trinity Episcopal Church in Independence said the bride was beautiful, and the minister added that he had never seen such a happy groom.

Bess and Harry Truman moved into the Wallace's large home in Independence with Bess's mother, her grandmother, and Bess's youngest brother. Mrs. Wallace still disapproved of Harry Truman, the one-time farmer. If the idea of living with his mother-in-law ever bothered Harry, he never let it be known.

Out of the army and married, Harry had to decide what he was going to do to earn a living. He did not want to go back to farming because there was little chance of making a good living year after year. With a wife to support, and no special skills, Harry tried to figure out what he was going to do.

He soon had an idea. Truman remembered the days in Oklahoma when he and his friend, Eddie Jacobson, ran a successful canteen, or army store,

Harry Truman's wedding party. Bess is standing to the right of Harry.

together. He and Jacobson decided to open a men's clothing store in Kansas City. Many of their army friends from the 129th Field Artillery lived in the area, and they felt certain that their friends would want to buy their clothes from two old army buddies.

Truman and Jacobson found a large corner store across the street from a busy hotel in the center of Kansas City. They both agreed that it would be a fine location for their business. Harry collected his share of the money for the venture by selling his interest in the family farm. The "Truman & Jacobson" store was in business. Just as they had expected, many friends from their army days came by to swap war stories, and stayed long enough to select something from their fine stock of ties, shirts, pants, and hats.

"Truman & Jacobson" did a whopping $70,000 in sales that first year, and bought more goods with their profits. In an ordinary business year this might have worked out fine, but 1922 was no ordinary business year. The bottom dropped out of prices. Clothes that Truman and Jacobson had paid a good price for early in the year were now worth much less.

Business people everywhere hoped that the economy would improve. Instead, conditions grew

Harry Truman (front left) and some of his friends at the Truman & Jacobson haberdashery, or clothing store, in Kansas City, Missouri.

worse. The partners' friends still came around the store, but now they were more likely to ask for a loan than to pick out a shirt or fancy pair of socks. The two disappointed store owners faced up to the truth—they were losing so much money each day that they would have to go out of business.

Even though many other businesses went bank-rupt and did not have to pay their debts, Eddie and Harry refused to take the easy way out. Instead, they returned the clothes to the wholesalers, and promised to pay off their debts. It took Harry fif-teen years to pay the $12,000 that he still owed, but he stuck to his word.

The future did not look promising for Harry Truman, but he was not a quitter.

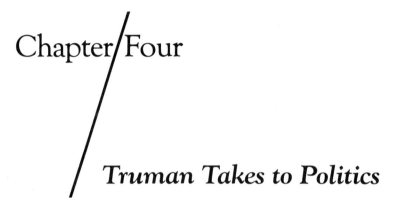

Chapter/Four

Truman Takes to Politics

At age thirty-eight, Harry Truman was looking for a decent, honest living. He began to think that this might be a good time to run for a political office. Politics had been on Harry's mind for a long time. His father had been a strong Democrat, and, as a little boy, Harry had trailed behind his father at Democratic party meetings. Years later, when John Truman took a job with the Democratic party, he let young Harry act as his secretary. Harry eventually began to attend political meetings on his own.

When Harry was overseas in the army, the soldiers in Company D would sometimes hear Captain Harry sound off about how he might run for Congress to make sure army officers did the right things. Though it may have been "just talk" then, Harry Truman was serious about running for office now.

One of the soldiers who listened to Captain Harry's ideas was Jim Pendergast. Jim's father, Mike Pendergast, and his uncle, Tom Pendergast, were active in Missouri politics in those days. The "Pendergast machine," as the political group was called, had ways of electing—or rejecting—certain candidates in the state.

Powerful political machines had operated in Missouri for years. They would choose a candidate and make sure that candidate was elected to office. Once "their man" was in office, the political machines could continue to influence Missouri politics in ways that best suited their own needs.

When Mike Pendergast heard that Truman was considering a step into politics, he was very interested in helping him. As it happened, the Pendergast machine was not happy with one of the three county judges in Jackson County. These politicians were looking for a loyal Democrat who had roots in farming and who was well known around the Kansas City area. Harry Truman had been a farmer for over ten years, and he knew many people—especially farmers and ex-soldiers.

Truman agreed to accept Pendergast's support

and decided to run for county judge. He felt that a good politician needed to be good at sizing up an opponent, figuring out the issues that the voters are concerned about, and meeting people. Harry thought he would do well at all three.

Traveling all over the county, Truman rang doorbells and gave speeches. He was not a good public speaker—his voice was flat, and he looked as though he were frightened to death. One listener said that he put audiences to sleep. Yet, somehow, his sincerity came through. Scattered through the audiences were people who knew Harry—farmers, Masons, relatives on either his or his wife's side, and old army buddies who remembered Captain Harry. Usually, friends and relatives in the audience cheered and clapped loudly despite Truman's stumbling voice.

Harry Truman was elected county judge of the eastern district of Jackson County, Missouri, in 1922. The three-man board of judges in the county had nothing to do with the legal system—they were in charge of constructing and maintaining county roads, parks, bridges, hospitals, and all other county buildings.

When Truman first took office, the men who bid on jobs for building county roads were surprised by the new county judge's ideas. Certain

Judge Truman signs county checks with multiple machine.

builders had been charging large sums of money for poorly built, cheap roads, and pocketing the extra money for themselves. Harry Truman would have none of this. He made sure that quality roads were built at a reasonable cost.

By the end of his term, Judge Truman felt quite satisfied with what he had accomplished. However, for Truman, the birth of his daughter, Margaret, was the most exciting event. Soon after Mary Margaret Truman was born on February 17, 1924, her doting father was doing everything he could to spoil her. No matter how busy he was, he never let anything interfere with his interest in and love for his daughter. When Margaret was young and Truman had to be away from home, he would close his many letters to Bess with a heartfelt, "and be sure and kiss my baby."

As the 1924 election approached, Truman hoped to be re-elected to office. But a split in the Democratic party and opposition from the Ku Klux Klan stood in the way of his re-election. The Klan was at its peak in the 1920s as a powerful political force. The group was against anyone it considered to be "un-American," including blacks, immigrants, Jews, and Roman Catholics.

Truman made a clean break with the Klan early in his political career when he angrily refused to promise that he would not hire Catholics if he were elected to the county court. The Klan was furious, and even threatened to kill Truman. After this incident, Truman surprised members of the Klan by interrupting one of their meetings to call them "a bunch of cheap un-American fakers" for labeling themselves as "Independent Democrats." The Klan got even in 1924 by launching a vicious campaign to defeat Truman in the election. Truman was not re-elected as county judge.

Though Truman was now out of office, he was not idle. He reorganized the Automobile Club of Kansas City, became president of the National Old

Trails Association, and vice-president of a savings and loan institution that he helped to start. In addition to these activities, he enrolled in Kansas City Law School because he felt that any public official should have a law degree.

He never had the chance to complete his degree. In 1926, Jackson County needed help. The roads were a crumbling mess, and the government was corrupt and in debt. The Pendergasts wanted Truman back in politics, and Truman was more than ready. He was elected to a key position as presiding judge in 1926 and spent the next eight years fighting corruption, pulling the government out of debt, building solid roads, and serving as president of the Greater Kansas City Planning Association.

Although Truman was very busy during these years, he always made time for his family. He enjoyed watching Margaret grow up, and he loved to tease her. Throughout his years as a politician, Truman was worried that someone might try to kidnap his only child. His politics had made some people angry, and the Klan still held a grudge against him.

Judge Truman had a real scare when Margaret was in the first grade. A teacher at Margaret's school phoned the Trumans to tell them that a man—someone she had never seen before—was at

Harry Truman's four-year-old "little darling" rides her tricycle in Independence, Missouri.

Presiding Judge Harry Truman sits in the center, with the district judges to either side of him and the county clerks standing in back of him.

the school saying he was supposed to take "Mary Truman" home. She grew suspicious when the man asked for Mary instead of Margaret—Mary was Margaret's first name, but no one ever called her that. The Trumans called the state police and raced to the school, but by the time they arrived, the man was gone. The family picked Margaret up from school for the rest of the year.

As 1934 drew to a close, Harry Truman had a decision to make. Presiding judges usually served only two four-year terms, and Truman's time was almost up. At the age of fifty, what was he going to do? He hoped to step into a higher political office, but that depended on whether or not Pendergast would back him. That didn't look promising, since Pendergast had not supported him when he wanted to run for the House of Representatives.

Truman got quite a surprise when Tom Pendergast asked him to run, not for the House of Representatives, but for the U.S. Senate. Why had Pendergast changed his mind? He had asked three other men to run for the Senate before he asked Truman, and each one of them had said no. Truman was the fourth choice!

Within two days, Truman accepted the Pendergast backing for a Missouri seat in the Senate, and began campaigning with his usual energy. He criss-crossed the state by car, visiting more than a dozen towns each day. In all, he visited more than half of Missouri's 114 counties. Truman was at his best meeting and talking to farmers or people from small towns. He tried to convince them to vote for him by reminding them of his experiences as a farmer, a soldier, a businessman, and a county judge.

On election day, Truman received more votes than any other candidate who ran in the Democratic primary. Now he had to run against the winner of the Republican primary. In Missouri, however, the Democratic primary winner was sure to win because Democrats far outnumbered Republicans. Harry Truman would be the new senator from the state of Missouri!

For the most part, the Trumans were thrilled by the news. Young Margaret, however, was horrified when she was told that the family would be moving to Washington, D.C., within a few weeks. She and her best friend cried for two days.

When the Trumans arrived in Washington, they were shocked to discover how expensive it was to rent a house or an apartment. They finally rented a small, four-room apartment—quite a switch from the fourteen-room house in Missouri!

Bess and Margaret decided to live half of the year in Washington, D.C., and half in Independence. Every June, Harry and the family would pack all their belongings in the car and drive the long stretch to Missouri. Back in Washington, Harry Truman was often lonely and miserable during those long periods spent without his wife and daughter. He visited Independence when he could, but he could not afford to make frequent trips. Instead, he threw himself into his work as a senator.

Although Truman was determined to do his best, his first days in the Senate were not pleasant ones. Many politicians feared that as a senator he would be under the control of the Pendergast po-

Margaret and Bess with Judge Truman.

litical machine that helped to elect him, and that he would not do what was best for the people of Missouri. Some of his fellow senators called him a Pendergast "stooge" and "errand boy." As far as these senators were concerned, he had been elected by a crooked political machine.

Truman, however, would have nothing to do with what he called "dirty politics." Though the criticism bothered him, he decided that the best thing to do was to proceed with his work. A senator told him, "You can be a show horse or a work horse." Harry had worked hard all his life, and he had no intention of changing now.

One of Truman's first tasks in the Senate was to direct an investigation of railroad finances as a member of the Senate Interstate Commerce Committee. For many years, the government had given railroad companies subsidies, or large sums of money, to build and improve their railroads. Truman had reason to believe that the owners of the railroads were using some of the money to "line their own pockets," and he wanted this stopped. He and a number of other senators worked to pass a law to do just that.

In time, Truman's fellow senators found him to be a friendly, likable man with common sense. They also noticed that he worked hard to research

Senate issues and to keep himself well informed. Although he slowly gained the respect of the Senate, many politicians and the Missouri newspapers predicted that Harry Truman would not be re-elected for a second term. The Pendergast machine that had helped to place him in office was now in ruins.

When Truman called a meeting of friends to support him for re-election, many of them did not even show up. When a friend told Harry he did not stand a chance, he answered, "At least I'll get two votes," meaning from himself and Bess.

Although Truman was ignored by many politicians and had little money for a campaign, he pushed ahead the only way he knew how. He traveled up and down the state of Missouri meeting all the people he could. His speeches were still dull and lifeless, but there was something about him that the people sensed—and liked. He was folksy, corny, confident, smiling, honest, sincere, and—perhaps most important of all—he seemed like one of them.

The campaign of 1940 was the toughest one Truman had ever faced. But Harry Truman fooled the so-called experts—he won the election. Six years before, when the new senator from Missouri had entered the Senate chambers for the first time, he was greeted with ugly whispers and snubs. This time, as Harry Truman walked to his seat, the senators rose to their feet and applauded.

What a difference six years has made, Truman thought. Still, he could not begin to imagine just how different the next few years would be.

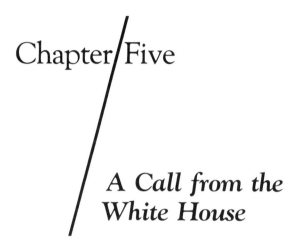

Chapter/Five

A Call from the White House

"I am at last doing the thing I most want to do in all the world."

This is the way Truman described his work as he began his second term in the Senate. At this time, most Americans outside of Missouri had never heard of Harry Truman. His fellow senators, though, knew that he was one of the hardest-working lawmakers in the Senate, which was all that mattered to Truman. Nothing would make him happier than staying in the Senate for the rest of his life.

Early in Senator Truman's second term, Bess and Margaret moved to Washington, D.C., to stay. Margaret's parents decided that she should have a full year at Washington's Gunston Hall and get her

Truman as a U.S. senator from Missouri in 1942.

diploma. Margaret, Bess, and Bess's mother loaded the car and moved to the capital. In time, Bess Truman joined the Senate office staff as a paid mail sorter to help out the family.

One morning, in 1940, Harry Truman sat reading the mail in his Senate office. As he unfolded one letter and began to read, his eyes narrowed in deep concern. The author of the letter claimed that the army was wasting a tremendous amount of money in building an army camp in Missouri.

At the time, the United States was preparing for a possible war. World War I had weakened European countries and left them vulnerable to attack. In the 1920s and 1930s, dictatorships seeking power and territory had begun to form in Germany, the Soviet Union, Italy, and Japan.

World War II began on September 1, 1939, when German troops crashed through Poland's defenses with tanks and dive bombers. Two days later, Great Britain and France, who were allies of Poland, declared war on Germany. By 1940, German forces under the leadership of Adolf Hitler, were conquering European countries with alarming speed. Although the U.S. government had announced its neutrality, the country had to prepare its defenses.

Millions of young Americans would soon be

drafted into the armed services. Factories switched from making peacetime goods to making war goods. The U.S. government was spending millions of dollars to strengthen the military. Truman wanted to find out if the government was spending it wisely.

Harry Truman passed on his concerns in a letter to the War Department. The issue might have ended there if the War Department had simply told the senator that they would look into the matter. Instead, the War Department told him, in effect, to mind his own business. Truman refused—saving money for the taxpayer would always be his business.

Before the War Department knew what was happening, the junior senator from Missouri was traveling from one army base to another, from one war plant to another, from one construction site to another—sticking his nose into army business everywhere. This was the same method he had used as county judge, when he inspected Jackson County buildings, checked roads, and examined costs. Only this time, Truman's car traveled from Florida, across the South to Texas, north to Nebraska, and back through Michigan. In all, he covered seventeen states.

When he returned to Washington, D.C., Truman told his fellow senators that the trip was an "eye opener" and that someone had to stop the terrible waste and inefficiency. After hearing Truman's report, the Senate agreed, and set up a committee to investigate the National Defense Program. Harry Truman was picked to head the committee.

The Truman Committee, as it came to be called, discovered that too much waste and "dumb-headedness" existed in many of the peacetime army programs. Then, on December 7, 1941, when Japan attacked the U.S. Navy base at Hawaii's Pearl Harbor, the United States entered the war against the Axis Powers of Japan, Germany, and Italy. Suddenly, the Truman Committee became more important than ever as the armed forces shifted gears to prepare for war.

Over the next few years, Harry Truman and his committee made some startling discoveries. In one factory, airplane engine parts were made incorrectly. At an army camp, construction workers were standing around doing nothing while the cost for building the camp increased. The government was wasting billions of dollars at army bases, shipyards, munition depots, and aircraft factories. The committee urged the government to take action to stop the wasteful spending.

Soon, the glare of publicity began to fall on the

committee's chairman—the very senator who was not particularly interested in publicity. In 1943, *Time* magazine published a cover story on Truman's committee. All of this media attention might have ended with some good publicity for the Senate if things were not beginning to stir inside the Democratic party. As the 1944 Democratic Convention drew near, the leading politicians in the party told President Roosevelt that they were not happy with Vice-President Henry Wallace. The vice-president was not popular with lawmakers, and he had made too many other enemies.

The Democratic party leaders started looking for someone to run in place of Henry Wallace. What about James Byrnes from South Carolina? they asked. He had been a senator, an associate justice of the Supreme Court, and the "right hand man" of President Roosevelt. But labor leaders did not want him, and that would cost the party too many votes. How about someone the labor leaders would like, someone who could attract southern votes as well as labor votes? How about Harry Truman?

When Harry Truman learned that the Democratic party leaders were interested in having him run for vice-president, he was stunned. He liked his job in the Senate, and wanted to stay there.

Truman did his best to say no. Then, President Roosevelt made it clear that, as "commander in chief," he wanted Harry Truman as his running mate. "Captain Harry" reluctantly went along with the orders of his commander.

The choice of vice-president was very important, especially in 1944, because President Roosevelt was very ill. If the president were to die in office, the vice-president would have to take his place. The Democratic party leaders believed that Truman would be an excellent candidate for this position. His work in the Senate—on the Truman Committee in particular—convinced them that Truman was their man.

When the campaign began, Truman was not well known, but that did not seem to matter much to the American public. Since President Roosevelt was still very popular after twelve years in office, Roosevelt and Truman easily defeated Republican nominees Thomas E. Dewey and John Bricker. On January 20, 1945, Roosevelt and Truman were sworn in as president and vice-president of the United States.

That day, Harry Truman called his ninety-two-year-old mother. "Did you hear my inauguration on the radio?" he asked.

"Yes," his mother answered, "I heard it all

A busy vice-president at his desk in 1945.

right. Now you behave yourself up there, Harry. You behave yourself."

"I will, Mama," the vice-president answered.

A few months later, on April 12, 1945, Harry Truman took his usual early morning walk. Then he went to the Senate building where, as vice-president, he presided over the Senate. The day's session was dull, and Truman was relieved when it was over. He went to the office of a congressman where some other members of Congress were going to relax and exchange stories. As soon as he entered the room, Truman was told that the White House had called. When he telephoned the White

House, the voice at the other end told him to come right over.

Truman rushed back to his office to pick up his hat. He had no idea why the White House had sent for him. When he arrived, he learned that President Roosevelt had died.

Two days later, Harry Truman wrote a letter to his mother and sister in Grandview.

Dear Mamma and Mary,
   . . .It was the only time in my life, I think, that I felt as if I'd had a real shock. I had hurried to the White House to see the President, and when I arrived, I found I was the President. No one in the history of our country ever had it happen to him just that way. . . .
   Lots of love from your very much worried son and bro.

                Harry

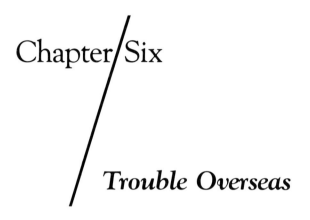

Chapter/Six

Trouble Overseas

When Harry Truman first took office as president, many people were curious to see how he would handle the job. They soon found out. Truman began his working day early in the morning, and did not end it until late at night. He saw three times as many people as the ailing Roosevelt had. He had a way of tackling every task head on; instead of putting off a decision, he wrestled with each problem until he found an answer that satisfied him.

Truman soon gained a reputation as a spry, energetic, hard-working, no-nonsense, fact-finding president with his own style of decision-making: talk to the right people, listen carefully, and read as much as possible. He believed that once he had made a decision, he should never look back.

President Truman's official first-term presidential photograph.

A plaque on the president's desk read "The Buck Stops Here." In the old days of the West, a piece of ivory made from the antlers of a buck (a male deer) was placed in front of a card player when it was his turn to deal. If the player did not want to deal, he simply "passed the buck" on to the person next to him, who could either deal the cards—or pass the buck again.

In time, "passing the buck," meant passing on the blame or responsibility to someone else. Truman believed that as long as he was president, he would take full responsibility for every important decision.

Truman had many decisions to make during his first few months in office. He had been president just over three weeks when, on May 7, 1945— with Allied armies closing in on Germany from the west, and Soviet troops entering from the east— Germany surrendered. Now the guns and cannons that had roared across the battlefields of Europe since September 1939 were finally silent. World War II had ended in Europe, but the United States remained at war with Japan.

A few months after Germany's surrender, Truman boarded the cruiser *Augusta* and sailed to his first foreign policy meeting in Potsdam, a city outside of Berlin, Germany. This conference would be a severe test for a politician who had no real experience in dealing with international politics. Truman, however, felt confident that his strong grasp of history and human nature would serve him well. "The only thing new in the world," Truman was fond of saying, "is the history you don't know."

Truman was reluctant to meet with other Allied leaders at Potsdam. He was struggling with the issue of how to get Japan to surrender, and he didn't have all of the facts yet. American scientists in the top secret Manhattan Project had been working hard to produce the atomic bomb. If the results were successful, the bomb might be a way to end the war with Japan quickly. And, if he knew the results, negotiating at the conference might be easier. Still, he could not put off going to the conference.

At Potsdam, Truman met with Winston Churchill, the prime minister of Great Britain, and Joseph Stalin, the premier of the Soviet Union. During the Potsdam Conference, the three leaders discussed many issues including the future of postwar Germany, new territorial boundaries in Europe, and how to force Japan to surrender.

Reminding the other two leaders how important it was "not to repeat the mistakes we made in the peace settlements of World War I," Truman suggested that they set up a council of foreign ministers that would meet to solve some of the postwar problems in Europe.

Early in World War II, Franklin Roosevelt had taken steps toward creating a worldwide peace organization. On June 26, 1945, representatives of fifty nations, including Great Britain, the Soviet Union, and the United States, met at the San Francisco Conference to sign the United Nations Charter.

At Potsdam, the Allied leaders were trying

At the Potsdam Conference, President Harry Truman sits with Prime Minister Winston Churchill of Great Britain (left) and Premier Joseph Stalin (right).

to organize the chaos left in the wake of World War II. Once postwar details were cleared up, the United Nations would try to make sure world peace would not be shattered again.

Truman had spoken to Churchill on the phone before, but they met face-to-face for the first time at Potsdam. Truman reported that he had an instant liking for the British prime minister "who had done so much for his own country and for the Allied cause." He found Churchill to be charming and clever. Yet, he mentioned in a letter that "he gave me a lot of hooey about how great my country is and how he loved Roosevelt and how he intended to love me, etc., etc.. . .I am sure we can get along if he doesn't try to give me too much soft soap."

Truman was also impressed with Stalin the first time he met him. "I talked to him straight from the shoulder," Truman reported, "and I felt that we could reach an agreement that would be satisfactory to the world and to ourselves."

While Truman was at the Potsdam Conference, he received the news that the first atomic bomb had been successfully tested. In a desolate part of Alamogordo, New Mexico, a gigantic atomic explosion had blasted the ground high into the sky. Truman wrote in his diary, "We have discovered the most terrible bomb in the history of the world. It seems to be the most terrible thing ever discovered."

Truman told Churchill and Stalin about the success of the atomic bomb test. Stalin did not show a great deal of interest, possibly because his spies had already informed him of the United States' atomic bomb project.

After consulting with his advisers, Truman made the decision to drop an atomic bomb on Japan. He gave Japan a general warning to surrender, but the warning did not specifically mention an atomic bomb. When Japan did not surrender, Truman gave the order. The first atomic

bomb in the history of the world fell on the city of Hiroshima on August 6, 1945. Even though the bomb killed seventy thousand Japanese and destroyed the city, Japan did not surrender. Three days later, a second atomic bomb fell on Nagasaki, killing thirty thousand more people. On August 14, 1945, the Japanese finally agreed to end the war.

Truman never doubted that he made the right decision to drop the atomic bombs on Japan. "I did not hesitate to order the use of bombs on military targets," said Truman. "I wanted to save half a million boys on our side, and as many on their side. I never lost any sleep over my decision."

Winston Churchill later wrote, ". . .the decision whether or not to use the atomic bomb to compel the surrender of Japan was never even an issue. There was unanimous, automatic, unquestioned agreement around our table; nor did I ever hear the slightest suggestion that we should do otherwise."

For many, the atomic bomb issue was more complicated. Some people questioned whether it was really necessary to drop the bombs. Shouldn't the United States have warned Japan about the bomb first and given the country a chance to surrender? they asked. Couldn't the U.S. government

The first atomic bomb test, referred to as the Trinity, takes place in the New Mexico desert.

have demonstrated the bomb on a deserted island first? Were more lives really saved by ending the war quickly with the bombs? Weren't the Japanese badly beaten already? Was dropping the bombs worth the huge loss of lives and the beginning of an age of nuclear weaponry?

Most of these questions, however, were asked after the bombs had been dropped. At the time, Japan still had a large army and was determined to keep on fighting. The United States saw the bomb as a quick way to end the war and to save the lives of both American and Japanese people. Japan's surrender marked the end of World War II, but it was not the end of world problems. For President Truman and other world leaders, rebuilding the war-torn countries and reaching decisions about other postwar problems would not be easy.

Chapter/Seven

A Fighting President

After the Potsdam Conference, dealing with the Soviet Union became more and more difficult. Although Truman was eager to maintain friendly relations with Stalin, he became alarmed when the Communists began taking over countries in eastern Europe.

Early in World War II, Germany had attacked the Soviet Union and pushed deep into Soviet territory. Later, the Soviet Union had pushed the Germans out, then rolled through the countries in eastern Europe.

Once Soviet troops entered Poland, Bulgaria, Romania, Austria, Czechoslovakia, and the eastern part of Germany, these areas fell under Soviet control. Even after the war ended, the Soviets were not willing to lessen their control. Gradually, the Soviet Union established Communist governments in these satellite countries. Great Britain and the United States could do little to protect these nations without going to war.

When the Soviet Union began to threaten the governments of Greece and Turkey, President Truman decided that the United States would have to take action to defend them. Because he did not want communism to spread to other countries of the world, Truman established what came to be called the "Truman Doctrine." The Truman Doctrine declared that the United States would come to the aid of any country threatened by a totalitarian regime (such as a Communist government).

The Truman Doctrine marked a real change in American foreign policy. Before World War II, the United States had tried to avoid getting involved in protecting other countries. However, Truman realized that after World War II, the United States was the only country in the world strong enough to stand up against the Soviet Union. Truman did not want to interfere in the Soviet Union itself or in other Communist countries—he wanted to protect other countries from the spread of communism.

The president urged Congress to set aside hundreds of millions of dollars in military and economic aid for Greece and Turkey. As a result, these two countries remained independent, and did not fall under the influence of the Soviet Union.

After almost six years of war, most of the countries of western Europe—France, Great Britain, Germany, the Netherlands, and Belgium—were weak and in ruins. Homes, farms, and factories were destroyed. The land needed planting and harvesting so that the people could be fed. These countries, in their weakened conditions, were targets for Communist takeovers.

Truman asked Congress for billions of dollars to help the western European countries rebuild. Once these countries gained strength, they would be able to support and defend themselves. Congress agreed to provide these funds under the European Recovery Program, better known as the Marshall Plan, and named after Truman's secretary of state, George C. Marshall. When a White House aide suggested calling the new policy the "Truman Plan," Truman said, "Are you crazy? If we sent it up to that Republican Congress with my name on it, they'd tear it apart. . . ."

The Marshall Plan worked well. When the first loads of food, machinery, and other products arrived from America, Europeans felt hopeful. Slowly, with years of hard work, the countries of west-

Harry Truman and George Marshall shake hands.

ern Europe recovered from the devastation of the war.

Still, the trouble was not over in Europe. With the defeat of Germany in 1945, the Allied nations had agreed to divide Germany into four parts. Great Britain, France, and the United States occupied their own sections in the western part of Germany, and the Soviet Union occupied the eastern part. Berlin, the German capital, was divided between the four nations, but lay entirely within Soviet-occupied East Germany. Roads, rails, airways, and waterways through East Germany connected West Germany with Berlin.

On a June day in 1948, Soviet soldiers, who ordinarily observed trucks filled with different products roll over the highway to Berlin, ordered the trucks to stop and turn back. Later, trains and canal boats heading for Berlin were also forced to turn around. The Soviets had set up a blockade to keep out all products coming from the west. They wanted to squeeze out Great Britain, France, and the United States. If supplies could not be brought in, Berlin would be forced to turn to the Soviet Union for help, and would then fall under the influence of the Soviet Union.

President Truman knew he had a serious problem. The United States could leave Berlin to the

Communists, but that would leave other parts of
Europe open to the threat of communism as well.
Ordering trucks to Berlin with an armed escort
would risk war with the Soviet Union. President
Truman had a difficult decision to make, and the
decision could not wait long—the people in Berlin
had only a thirty-day supply of food.

Truman studied the situation carefully. At last
he discovered a loophole that would allow him to
bypass the blockade. The Soviets controlled the
roads and water routes into Berlin, but there was
one small airstrip located in Allied-occupied West
Berlin. The Allies could fly in supplies to the Berliners without risking a war with the Soviets.

A few days after the blockade began, the president gave the order for American transport planes
to load up with coal, food, and other products, and
fly directly to Berlin. He would show the world
that the United States was not deserting Berlin!

When the "Berlin airlift" began, most people,
including some American generals, did not believe
it would work. Was it possible to send in enough
supplies to feed and take care of a city of more than
two million people? Nothing like it had ever been
done before. Yet, by the end of the summer, American and British planes were bringing in four thousand tons of food a day, and planes were landing

Planes line up, waiting to be loaded with supplies for the Berliners.

every forty-five seconds. The people of Berlin were surviving the Berlin Blockade.

In May 1949, eleven months after it had begun, the Soviets gave up the blockade. The experts who had told Truman the airlift would not work were wrong.

The Soviets had been defeated this time, but the western countries wanted to protect themselves from further Communist aggression. In 1949, twelve nations signed the North Atlantic Treaty. Under this agreement, if any one of the member nations were attacked, all of the other nations would come to its defense. For the first time, the United States joined a peacetime alliance that committed it to fight in Europe. Later, in 1950, the North Atlantic Treaty Organization (NATO) was formed to carry out the principles outlined in the 1949 treaty.

Not all of President Truman's attention was focused on international affairs. He had many problems to deal with in the United States as well.

Chapter/Eight

On the Home Front

Harry Truman leaned forward at his desk and stared coldly at the two labor leaders sitting uncomfortably across from him. The president of the United States made no effort to hide his anger. "If you think I'm going to sit here and let you tie up this whole country," he said, "you're crazy."

The railroad union was getting ready to call a strike, and Truman had invited the two men to his office, hoping they would change their minds. Since so many of the nation's goods were shipped by train in 1946, Truman knew a strike meant trouble. The president had considered these men his friends when he was a senator working to improve conditions for the railroad workers in America. In fact, many American labor leaders had encouraged the Democratic party to choose Harry Truman as the vice-presidential nominee. Their positions were different now—the railroad workers wanted more money, and they were ready to strike for it.

One of the labor leaders cleared his throat. "Mr. President, we've got to go through with it."

Harry Truman stood up. "You've got just forty-eight hours to reach a settlement," he announced. "If you don't, I'm going to take over the railroads in the name of the government."

No president had ever taken over the railroads in peacetime before, but that did not stop Truman from making the threat. A few days later, the president stood before the House of Representatives urging Congress to pass a law that would allow the government to take control of the railroads. Truman had just started his speech when someone handed him a note. He glanced down, read the message, and then broke into a broad grin. "Gentlemen," he said, "the strike has been settled." The congressmen applauded. Although Truman had won the fight to keep the trains going, it had cost him the friendship and support of many labor leaders.

Truman did not believe in doing things just to please people. He wanted to do what he believed

Truman speaks to Congress, soon after becoming president.

was best for the country. Though this approach did not make him popular, it was the way he had always worked—and he was not about to change because he was the president.

During his first term as president, Truman faced many political battles. After World War II, in 1946, almost two million workers went on strike. Business people clamored for more profits, and workers demanded higher wages.

Americans also demanded certain items that were in short supply during the war. In wartime, meat and sugar had been rationed so that citizens could only buy a certain amount each week. Prices and wages had been controlled by law. Because American factories had been making products for the war, Americans could not make purchases such as new automobiles and new homes. Once the war ended, though, Americans were no longer willing to make these sacrifices.

President Truman tried to explain to the American people that if all government controls on profits, prices, and wages were suddenly stopped, too many people would be trying to buy a small amount of goods. Then the price of these goods would skyrocket, and this sudden rise in prices—called inflation—would be bad for the country. However, the American public was not listening to Harry Truman—perhaps because they saw a plain-looking man with a flat voice trying to persuade them, instead of the glamorous, dynamic Franklin D. Roosevelt.

The president also faced opposition within the government. When he urged the members of Congress to pass laws that would give blacks more civil rights, they took very little action. Living in Missouri had taught Truman how blacks were treated, especially in the South. "Jim Crow" laws—passed after the Civil War—kept blacks separate from whites. Restaurants, theaters, and drinking fountains had signs that said *Whites Only*. Black people and white people had to attend separate schools and sit in separate sections on trains or buses.

Sometimes a black accused of a serious crime was taken away by a mob of angry people and lynched before a trial could take place. Black people were supposed to have the right to vote, but certain laws kept them away from the polls. For example, some southern states had a poll tax that only white voters could afford to pay.

President Truman made it clear that he thought racial discrimination in the legal system was wrong. He appointed a commission that worked to make sure blacks were treated fairly in industries with federal contracts, and he pushed to improve the way that blacks were treated in the military services. In a letter to an old friend, Truman wrote, "...I am asking for equality of opportunity for all human beings and, as long as I stay here, I am going to continue that fight."

Truman wanted a "fair deal" for all citizens. His so-called Fair Deal program was one of social reform—he tried to pass laws that would provide money for building homes, for insuring farmers' crops, and for providing more income to unemployed and poor people. Congress refused to pass most of the Fair Deal laws, but that did not keep Truman from trying.

The president had a heavy load to carry during his first term, but he rarely showed signs of strain or fatigue. Truman brought a great deal of energy to his job. He awoke at six A.M., looked over three or four newspapers, wrote some letters, and then—promptly at seven—began a brisk, before-breakfast walk. He zipped through the streets of Washington at a rapid 120 paces per minute with Secret Service men and a few reporters doing their best to keep up with him. By eight, a fresh Harry Truman was ready for a long working day.

As the American people were getting used to the Trumans, the Truman family was trying to adjust to being the nation's First Family. Truman once complained that being the president was like living in a fishbowl. However, he did enjoy being with people, and he adapted well to his public life.

Harry Truman's life had always centered on his wife and daughter. He thought of himself as a husband and father first, and then, as a president. Margaret, who was a twenty-one-year-old college student when Truman became president, seemed to enjoy the attention she received as a member of the First Family. She was launching her career as a professional singer.

Bess Truman, however, never felt comfortable in the public eye. She was an outgoing, intelligent

Truman relaxes with his family on a vacation in Key West, Florida, in 1948.

woman with a rich sense of humor. Early in her life she had found a warm circle of close friends and relatives in her hometown of Independence, Missouri. She longed to return to her private life. Bess fulfilled her obligations as a First Lady—greeting important people on special occasions, or serving as a hostess for foreign diplomats—but her heart was never in it.

As the 1948 presidential election approached, Harry Truman tried to decide whether or not to run. Bess did not want him to run, but she knew her husband well enough to know he would do what he believed was right. Harry Truman did not like the idea of quitting with so much of his work unfinished—many of his Fair Deal ideas had not been accomplished, and Soviet-style communism still threatened other parts of the world. Besides, it would be a challenge to run on his own, and not as the running mate of a very popular president. These were exactly the kinds of challenges that Bess's feisty husband could never turn down.

When Harry Truman announced that he would run for president, many important politicians in the Democratic party were disappointed. There is an expression, "To err is human," that is, to make a mistake, is human. Some newspapers mocked the president with the expression, "To err is Truman." At one time, only 23 percent of the people in answer to a poll said they thought he was doing a good job. Democrats, people in his own party, took a popular song, "I'm Just Wild About Harry," and turned it into a joke, singing, "I'm Just Mild About Harry." They did not think he had any chance of winning.

Many people dropped hints that perhaps he should not run. They might as well have tried to convince a stubborn Missouri mule.

Chapter/Nine

The Big Surprise

The six hundred Republican men and women who were jammed together in the fancy New York Roosevelt Hotel dining room—as well as the three hundred more Republicans who overflowed into the stairwells and lobby—were in a happy-go-lucky, joking mood. They had been working and waiting for this event—election night, November 2, 1948. The large blue banner draped across one end of the beautiful room proclaimed this to be the Republican victory party for the soon-to-be-elected president—Thomas E. Dewey. At last, after sixteen years, a Republican president was going to be in the White House!

For months, every American pollster, an expert who keeps track of how people decide to vote, had reported that Governor Thomas Dewey of New York would be elected president. The political newspaper reporters and respected magazines throughout the country—including *Time, Life,* and *Newsweek*—all claimed that Truman's days in the White House were numbered. Based on the predictions of the media, the Republican party workers who had come to celebrate victory had good reason to be confident.

Then, about seven-thirty, the first returns of the election came in. Truman was ahead! The people milling about the room looked a little puzzled. How could Truman be ahead? they asked.

Soon the Republicans began to laugh and shout encouragement to one another. These were, after all, only the early returns. At eight-thirty, Truman was even further ahead, but the Republicans kept on reassuring each other that Dewey would win. Everyone believed that Truman had too many things going against him to win this election.

For one thing, most of the important labor leaders were upset with the president because he had tried to stop them from striking. Some southern Democrats were angry at Harry Truman for standing up for civil rights for black Americans. These Democrats started a political party of their own, called the States' Rights Democratic, or Dixiecrat party, and nominated South Carolina governor Strom Thurmond as their candidate for president. Then, Henry Wallace, an earlier vice-president under Franklin D. Roosevelt, became the candidate for the Progressive party. Wallace decided to run for president because he did not approve of Truman's tough stand against the Soviet Union.

The Republicans at the Roosevelt Hotel believed that many citizens who ordinarily voted for the Democratic candidate would be voting for Strom Thurmond or Henry Wallace on election day. As the evening wore on, and as the Republicans eyed the results scribbled in chalk on the large board in front of the room, something very strange began to happen. Harry Truman was getting even further ahead! It did not seem possible, but his lead kept growing—and in some of the biggest and most important states.

Shocked and disappointed by the election results, some of the Republicans started to drift away. By midnight most of them had gone. There would be no Republican victory celebration that night.

The next morning, Americans awakened to the news that Harry Truman had pulled off the greatest political upset in presidential history. Truman received 24,105,587 votes to Dewey's 21,970,017

votes. Thurmond and Wallace received a little over
a million votes each—not enough to hurt Truman.
Truman won 303 of the 531 electoral votes. Some
newspapers were so certain that the early returns
would change that they had actually delivered newspapers with headlines announcing Dewey as the
new president. A few magazines—because they had
to go to press before election day—had articles
about "Our new president, Thomas Dewey."

Everyone wanted to know how Harry Truman
achieved a "political miracle." What turned the
campaign around for Harry Truman?

Perhaps it was what happened on an April
evening months before the elections. President Truman stood before the American Society of Newspaper Editors and read from a typewritten speech
that was also being broadcast on the radio. The
president droned on, sometimes reading too quickly or emphasizing the wrong words. He was his
usual, dull, uninspiring, speech-making self.

When the radio broadcast was over, Harry Truman put down the typed sheets in his hand, and
spoke off the cuff—without a typed speech or any
notes in front of him. The bored group of editors
suddenly perked up. Why, the speaker knew what
he was talking about! He was sincere, knowledge-
able, and inspiring. Truman spoke informally for

A smiling Harry Truman holds up a copy of the Chicago Tribune to a crowd at a train station in St. Louis, Missouri. The headline reads "Dewey Defeats Truman!"

twenty minutes. When he finished, the newspaper editors—even though most of them were not Truman supporters—broke into a rousing round of applause.

That lesson was not lost on Harry Truman. From then on, instead of reading prepared speeches, Truman spoke directly to the voters in his own old-fashioned, down-to-earth style. Americans began to listen to their straight-talking president.

Truman set forth his campaign strategy in a letter to his sister: "It will be the greatest campaign any president ever made. Win, lose, or draw, people will know where I stand." Harry Truman was right. He traveled 31,000 miles by train and gave about 350 speeches to over 12,000,000 people. There would never be another campaign like it— by 1952 candidates would turn to television to reach most American voters.

On the campaign train, Truman was up early in the morning and on the go until late at night, making speech after speech. In big cities, in small towns, or smaller "whistle stops"—places where a train stops only when a whistle signals that someone wants to get on or off—Harry Truman delivered his speeches.

Truman and his fellow politicians had worked out a routine. As the train drew to a stop and the

The Trumans return from a political trip during the 1948 presidential campaign.

local band blared out the "Missouri Waltz," an energetic-looking Harry Truman stepped onto the back platform. The crowd would push its way around the platform and greet the smiling president with cheers and whistles. Truman would then launch a brief speech aimed at convincing everyone present that he and the Democratic party would do what was best for common people like themselves.

Then, with a twinkle in his eye, Truman would introduce "the Boss." Bess would step out to loud cheers. "And, now," Truman would add, "I'd like you to meet the one who bosses the boss," and

Margaret Truman would step out onto the platform. The crowd loved it, and so did Harry Truman.

The president was at his best running a "rough-and-tough" campaign. He warned one group of voters that "If Republicans win, they'll tear you apart." He told some workers that if they were foolish enough to elect the Republicans, "You can expect to be hit by a steady barrage of body blows." He called Dewey "a man with a calculating machine where his heart ought to be."

When all the traveling, campaigning, and speech-making were finished, Harry Truman had convinced more than twenty-four million people that he and Senator Alben Barkley of Kentucky were the best candidates for president and vice-president of the United States.

For the first time, Harry Truman was a president elected by the people, and not someone who had come into the office by accident. The campaign had been a challenge and a success, but the excitement of victory would soon be overshadowed by trouble in the Far East.

Chapter/Ten

Leader in Crisis

"Mr. President, I have very serious news. The North Koreans have invaded South Korea!"

President Truman was spending a quiet evening with his family at his home in Independence, Missouri, on June 25, 1950, when Secretary of State Dean Acheson phoned with this message. The president wanted to fly back to Washington immediately, but Acheson suggested that he wait until they had a better picture of what was happening. Truman agreed.

This was grim news. Truman feared that a war in Korea could expand into a third world war. For years, Japan had ruled Korea, but when Japan surrendered to the Allies in 1945, Korea was supposed to become a free and independent country.

However, for a time, Soviet troops controlled the northern part of Korea, and U.S. troops occupied the southern part. Although this arrangement was only intended to be temporary, before long the Soviet Communists were in full control of the northern part of Korea. By 1950 the Soviet and American troops had left, and Korea was really two countries—Communist North Korea above the Thirty-eighth Parallel, and South Korea below it.

The day after Truman heard the news, he returned to Washington to meet with his top military officers and some of his cabinet members. He learned that thousands of North Korean troops were crossing the Thirty-eighth Parallel. Tanks, planes, and artillery were pounding the South Korean army. The fighting was heavy, and it looked as though the South Koreans would not be able to stop the invaders. Communist China, just to the north of Korea, as well as the Soviet Union, appeared to support the North Korean invasion. These invading troops were too well trained and too well equipped to be making such a strong military move on their own.

Determining the U.S. role in Korea was the most difficult issue the president would have to face during his second term in office. Truman believed that if the United States took no action in

Korea, other countries would think that they could not depend on the United States either. If he took a stand, Truman believed, it would warn the Communists against attempting further attacks.

On June 27, the president gave the order to send U.S. ships and planes stationed in Japan to Korea. He also asked the United Nations to request troops from other countries. Because the Soviet representative was absent and unable to veto the decision, the United Nations Security Council voted in favor of sending troops to Korea. In the meantime, the North Koreans continued their strong drive into South Korea until it looked as though the South Korean forces would be pushed right into the sea.

General Douglas MacArthur, the five-star general in charge of the United States armed forces in Korea, ordered an invasion far to the north, at a port called Inchon. The invasion caught the North Korean troops by surprise, and they were then pushed back to the Thirty-eighth Parallel.

Instead of stopping at the Thirty-eighth Parallel, MacArthur's troops continued north until they drew close to the Communist Chinese border. Truman was concerned that Chinese troops who had stayed out of the fighting would now strike back if MacArthur's forces came too close to the Chinese

President Truman shakes hands with General Douglas MacArthur after a 1950 conference on Wake Island in the North Pacific.

border. General MacArthur assured Truman that this would not happen.

MacArthur was wrong.

In late November 1950, three hundred thousand Chinese troops surprised the smaller American and South Korean forces with a massive attack that sent them reeling back. It was the darkest hour of the war for the American, South Korean, and U.N. forces. Then Lieutenant General Matthew Ridgway, an American officer, led his men in two offenses that stopped the Chinese advance. For the rest of the war, the armies battled near the Thirty-eighth Parallel.

Truman did not want the war to spread from Korea into China. He believed—and his civilian and military advisers in Washington agreed—that the cost in men and materials for such a war would be unbelievably high. Besides, Truman felt that a war with China would weaken the United States so much that the Soviet Union would be able to take over other European countries.

MacArthur, on the other hand, wanted American bombers to attack China even if it meant risking war. MacArthur believed the world would think the United States was a weak country if the military backed down. He was upset when he was told that he could not strike at China, and he kept telling news reporters that he thought this policy was wrong. Each time, Truman warned General MacArthur that his statements directly opposed U.S. government policy.

When MacArthur learned that the United States and the United Nations were going to propose a peace agreement with China, he did something very unusual. He told the Chinese that he, MacArthur, would negotiate with them, and that if they did not agree to his terms, he would see to it that their homeland was destroyed. Truman was angered by MacArthur's threat.

General MacArthur was a great American hero

who had been in charge of all of the Allied forces in the Far East during World War II. Truman knew that he would be harshly criticized if he took action against someone as popular as MacArthur. However, if MacArthur was excused for abusing his power as a general, other popular high-ranking military officers might also ignore presidential orders. The generals and admirals in Washington agreed with the president that something had to be done. On April 11, 1951, President Truman ordered that General MacArthur be "relieved of all of his duties."

Many Americans were enraged when they heard the news of MacArthur's firing. More than one newspaper pointed out that America's least popular president had fired America's most popular war hero. When he returned to the United States, MacArthur was given a hero's welcome. Truman stood his ground, confident he was right and that, in time, the American public would see it that way. Truman, and not General MacArthur, had been elected by the people to make these decisions. "Even Washington and Jefferson," Truman told a reporter years later, "kept warning the people against letting the generals give you too much advice."

After peace talks with the Chinese Commu-

nists began in July 1951, the fighting in Korea continued on a much smaller scale. As much as Truman wanted to, he was not able to end the war
during his term in office.

About this time, a strong feeling of anti-
communism was spreading throughout the United
States. The House Un-American Activities Committee claimed that a Communist spy ring existed
within the federal government. Truman thought
this idea was ridiculous.

To make matters worse, in 1949 the Soviets
exploded an atomic bomb. Many Americans believed that if the Soviets were rapidly developing
nuclear weapons, the United States and the rest of
the world would be in danger of a Communist take-
over. After much serious discussion, Truman decided that the United States would have to continue its nuclear research to match the power of the
Soviets.

At the time, scientists were discussing whether
or not to continue their research on the hydrogen
bomb, or H-bomb—one hundred to one thousand
times more destructive than the atomic bombs
dropped on Japan. Truman's decision to go ahead
with research on this bomb was the first step toward a nuclear arms race with the Soviet Union.

International politics had been unstable and

unpredictable for years. Truman was concerned about the security of the United States, but he also worried about his own family's security. He had good reason to be concerned. One afternoon, President Truman was jarred awake from a nap by the sound of gunfire. When he moved toward a window to find out what was going on, a Secret Service guard shouted a warning for the president to get back. Two Puerto Rican nationalists intent on reaching the president were trying to shoot their way through the entrance of Blair House, where the president and his family were staying while the White House was being remodeled.

For almost three minutes the two gunmen exchanged fire with Secret Service and police guards. One of the men actually reached the front door before he was stopped. When it was over, a guard and one gunman lay dead. The other gunman was captured. The two would-be assassins were part of a small group who were trying to win Puerto Rico's independence from the United States.

President Truman went about his duties the rest of the day as if nothing had happened. Later, Truman commented, "A president has to expect those things." A shocked American public seemed to be having more trouble than the president in accepting the violent attempt on Truman's life.

Truman takes a morning walk with Secret Service men and several plainclothesmen while visiting his home in Independence, Missouri.

As Truman's second term in office drew to a close, people began to wonder if Harry Truman would seek re-election once more. The Twenty-second Amendment to the Constitution states that a president can serve no more than two terms. Since the amendment was adopted while Truman was president, it did not apply to him.

Nevertheless, Truman told the American people he would not be a candidate for president. One day, Truman's press secretary, Charlie Ross, told the president he thought Truman would "rather be right than president."

Truman quickly answered, "Charlie, I would rather be anything than president." Eight years in office was enough.

Truman left office in January 1953. If he had any reason to wonder what the public thought of their plucky president after eight years, he would soon find out. When he and Bess arrived at the train station in Washington, D.C., to leave for Independence, a crowd of thousands was waiting for them. People in the crowd shouted best wishes and then joined in singing "Auld Lang Syne." As the train moved west toward Missouri, thousands of people stood at each stop and offered their best wishes to the former president. The town of Independence—home to Harry and Bess for over half a century—showed the warmest outpouring of love and respect. Ten thousand people jammed the railroad station, and another five thousand gathered by the Truman home to welcome the family.

Harry and Bess, their eyes misty, their voices choked with emotion, looked out at the railroad station crowd. From time to time over the years, the two of them had wondered if being in public office was worth all the hard work, pain, and heartaches. Harry and Bess looked out at the sea of friends from Independence. Now, they knew for sure that it was.

At long last, Bess and Harry were home again.

One afternoon, a few months after Harry Truman left the White House, he and a friend were driving down a quiet Missouri road when they saw a dozen hogs scampering on the pavement up ahead. Off to the side, a woman waved her arms frantically as she tried to get the hogs off the road and out of the way.

Harry Truman shouted to his friend behind the wheel to stop the car. As soon as the car stopped, he jumped out. With his friend directing oncoming cars around them, Truman proceeded to help the woman corral her hogs.

To a stranger, the sight of a man who was once

president of the United States trying to shoo some pigs off of a country road might have seemed strange. Yet, to anyone who lived around western Missouri, there was nothing unusual about the scene. Truman had spent the first fifty years of his life living and working in Missouri. No amount of working in Washington, D.C., was going to take the country out of Harry Truman.

When Harry, Bess, and Margaret returned to their home in Independence, they found that it had become a tourist attraction. People often drove by and took pictures of the house. Truman received more than seventy thousand letters during his first month out of office. The public was not ready to forget their recent president.

For Truman, retirement did not mean relaxation. He set up an office in Kansas City, where he answered thousands of letters, organized his papers for his memoirs, and made plans for the Harry S. Truman Library.

Truman was excited about the prospect of raising funds, choosing a site, and designing this library. Soon he became involved with every detail of the plans. The library would contain a replica of his White House office, a collection of souvenirs from his World War I days with Battery D, political cartoons from his two presidential terms, and a

President John F. Kennedy meets with Harry Truman in 1961.

series of rooms that instructed the public about the responsibilities of the U.S. president.

During the first few years of Truman's retirement, he traveled from California to England to New York—often for pleasure, sometimes to lecture at universities. He continued his active interest in politics and the Democratic party.

Family life was keeping Truman busy as well. Margaret married Clifton Daniel, a *New York Times* editor. In the next years, the retired president became a proud grandfather and enjoyed watching his four grandsons grow up. For years, Truman remained an energetic and active man. He died on

Harry and Bess Truman greet Margaret and their grandchildren at the Independence train station.

December 12, 1972, at eighty-eight years of age. He was buried in the Harry S. Truman Library's courtyard.

Harry Truman, born and raised in the nineteenth century, faced some of the twentieth century's greatest challenges with honesty, integrity, and a fighting spirit. His decisions reshaped U.S. foreign policy—dropping the bombs on Japan began the age of nuclear weaponry, and the Truman Doctrine and Marshall Plan marked new advances in the role of the United States in world affairs. The Berlin Blockade and the Korean War also tested and strengthened U.S. policy.

The president's ideas for the United States, such as the Fair Deal program, were often blocked by Congress. During his terms in office, he was criticized as "the worst president in history." Despite this opposition, Harry Truman never lost faith in himself, and in the belief that what he was doing was right. Today, he is remembered as one of the strongest and most capable leaders in the nation's history.

Appendix/

Major Events in Truman's Life

1884   Truman is born in Lamar, Missouri, on
            May 8

1902-06   Truman family moves from Indepen-
            dence, Missouri, to Kansas City, Missou-
            ri, in 1902; young Truman works as a
            bank clerk to help support his family

1906-17   Truman works on the family farm near
            Grandview, Missouri

1917-19   Truman serves as captain in France dur-
            ing World War I

1919   Truman marries Elizabeth "Bess" Virgin-
            ia Wallace on June 28

1919-22   Truman opens clothing store with Eddie Jacobson in Kansas City, Missouri

1923-25   Truman serves as judge in Jackson County, Missouri

1924   Truman's daughter, Mary Margaret Truman, is born on February 17

1927-35   Truman serves as presiding judge in Jackson County, Missouri

1935-44   Truman serves as U.S. senator from Missouri; he chairs Truman Senate Committee from 1941 to 1944

1944   President Franklin D. Roosevelt is elected to a fourth term; Harry Truman is elected as vice-president

1945   President Roosevelt dies in office on April 12; Truman sworn in as thirty-third president; Germany surrenders to Allies on May 7; World War II ends in Europe; Truman attends Potsdam Conference in Germany with Stalin and Churchill on July 17; Japan agrees to end war on August 14 after atomic bombs are dropped on Hiroshima and Nagasaki; United Nations is founded on October 24

1947   Truman announces the Truman Doctrine; George Marshall announces the Marshall Plan

1948   Truman asks Congress to pass various civil rights laws; Soviets begin the Berlin Blockade; Truman plans the Berlin airlift; Truman defeats Dewey in presidential election

1949   Truman delivers Fair Deal message to Congress; North Atlantic Treaty is signed; Soviets end Berlin Blockade

1950   North Atlantic Treaty Organization is formed; Truman announces the creation of the hydrogen bomb; Korean War begins; Chinese troops enter Korean War; Puerto Rican nationalists attempt to assassinate Truman

1951   Truman fires MacArthur

1953   Truman leaves office as Dwight Eisen-
        hower is sworn in as president; Truman
        and wife retire to Independence, Missou-
        ri; Korean War ends

1957   Harry S. Truman Library opens

1972   Truman dies on December 26

Selected Bibliography

Abels, Jules. *Out of the Jaws of Victory*. New York: Henry Holt and Company, 1959.

Cochran, Bert. *Harry Truman and the Crisis Presidency*. New York: Funk & Wagnall, 1973.

Daniels, Jonathan. *The Man of Independence*. New York: J.P. Lippincott, 1950.

Ferrell, Robert H. *Harry S. Truman and the Modern American Presidency*. Boston and Toronto: Little, Brown and Company, 1983.

Ferrell, Robert H. *Truman: A Centenary Remembrance*. New York: The Viking Press, 1984.

Gosnell, Harold F. *Truman's Crises: A Political Biography of Harry S. Truman.* Westport, CT: Greenwood Press, 1980.

Hedley, John Hollister. *Harry S. Truman: The "Little" Man From Missouri.* Woodbury, NY: Barron's, 1979.

Miller, Edward and Mueller, Betty Jean. *The Harry S. Truman Library.* New York: Meredith Press, 1966.

Miller, Merle. *Plain Speaking: An Oral Biography of Harry S. Truman.* New York: Berkley Publishing Corporation, distributed by G. P. Putnam's Sons, 1974.

Phillips, Cabell. *The Truman Presidency: The Story of a Triumphant Succession.* New York: Macmillan, 1966.

Robbins, Charles. *Last of his Kind: An Informal Portrait of Harry S. Truman.* New York: William Morrow and Company, 1979.

Truman, Harry. *The Autobiography of Harry S. Truman.* Edited by Robert H. Ferrell. Boulder: Colorado Associated University Press, 1980.

_____. *Dear Bess*. Edited by Robert H. Ferrell. New York and London: W. W. Norton, 1983.

_____. *Letters Home by Harry Truman*. Edited by Monte M. Poen. New York: G. P. Putnam's Sons, 1984.

_____. *Memoirs by Harry S. Truman, Volume One, Year of Decisions*. Garden City: Doubleday, 1955.

_____. *Memoirs by Harry S. Truman, Volume Two, Years of Trial and Hope*. Garden City: Doubleday, 1956.

_____. *Off the Record: The Private Papers of Harry S. Truman*. Edited by Robert H. Ferrell. New York: Harper and Row, 1980.

Truman, Margaret. *Harry S. Truman*. New York: William Morrow and Company, Inc., 1973.

Index